BEGINNING BLUEGRASS

Everything you need to know to become an accomplished performer of

Order No. AM 35213
US International Standard Book Number: 0.8256.2368.5
UK International Standard Book Number: 0.7119.0455.3

Exclusive Distributors:
Music Sales Corporation
257 Park Avenue South, New York, NY 10010 USA
Music Sales Limited
8/9 Frith Street, London W1V 5TZ England
Music Sales Pty. Limited
120 Rothschild Street, Rosebery, Sydney, NSW 2018, Australia

Printed in the United States of America by
Vicks Lithograph and Printing Corporation

Amsco Publications.
New York/London/Sydney/Cologne

Order No. AM 35213
International Standard Book Number: 0.8256.2368.5

Exclusive Distributors:
Music Sales Corporation
257 Park Avenue South, New York, NY 10010
Music Sales Limited
8/9 Frith Street, London W1V 5TZ England
Music Sales Pty. Limited
120 Rothschild Street, Rosebery, Sydney, NSW 2018, Australia

Printed in the United States of America by
Vicks Lithograph and Printing Corporation

Contents

To the Student

Bluegrass is an energetic and, at its best, a truly dazzling style of guitar playing. This book will lead you in a clear cut, step-by-step way from the basic chords, through the rudiments of the bluegrass style and into some very exciting music.

You'll learn all of the basic right- and left-hand techniques along with chord positions, runs, backup styles, and exciting solos to many standard bluegrass tunes. The tunes and the instruction are designed to acquaint you with the sound of good, authentic bluegrass as you learn to play it well, both technically and musically.

So, whether you're a beginner or a more experienced guitar student, *How to Play Bluegrass Guitar* can be extremely valuable to you. Even if bluegrass isn't your main interest, the skills it develops will provide a solid foundation for playing many other kinds of guitar music.

I hope this book helps make all of your musical experience more rewarding.

To the Teacher

In this book I've tried to present a simple and systematic approach to all aspects of bluegrass guitar playing without sacrificing the feel of real bluegrass music. *How to Play Bluegrass Guitar* can serve not only as a rich source of material to be used in lessons, but also as a well-organized guideline to the teacher. As such, it leaves considerable room for flexibility so that you can use it with your own individual teaching style at a pace beneficial to the particular student.

Feel free to supplement and enrich the text with your own insights. If a student is having particular difficulties, focus on the appropriate section of the book, and expand on it with some of your other teaching materials. Hopefully, *How to Play Bluegrass Guitar* will be a useful vehicle through which you can convey the tangibles and intangibles that stimulate a student's musical spirit.

Introduction

Bluegrass is a particular form of country music that uses mostly acoustic instruments. A full bluegrass band contains a guitar, bass, five-string banjo, mandolin, fiddle and sometimes a dobro.

The musical form was crystallized in the 40s and 50s with such personalities as Bill Monroe, Earl Scruggs, Lester Flatt, the Stanley Brothers, Jimmy Martin, Don Reno and Red Smiley, and Jim and Jesse McReynolds. It featured a driving rhythm, "high, lonesome" singing with tight vocal harmonies and some pretty fancy solos by the fiddle, banjo and mandolin.

In the early days, though there were a few exceptions, the guitar served mainly as a rhythm instrument. It's a latecomer to bluegrass as far as solo work is concerned, blossoming in the mid to late 60s with the rising popularity of Doc Watson and Clarence White. (Though Doc is not, strictly speaking, a bluegrass player, his style was very influential.) They provided a foundation for a whole generation of modern bluegrass guitar players. Since then, the guitar as a lead instrument has come a long way in a short time and is now accepted as an increasingly important part of bluegrass.

Listen to as much bluegrass music as you can. Knowing how the music sounds, you'll have a better idea of what you're working toward, and your playing will develop more rapidly in the right directions.

It will also help tremendously to play with other musicians when you feel that you're ready. Even as a beginner, feel free to try out what you learn with others at your own level.

Review of Chords

These are the basic chords we will use in this book. If you don't know some of them, you can learn them now, or look them up when you need them.

G
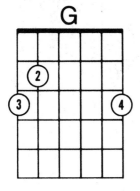

C
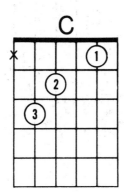

D
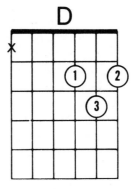

D7
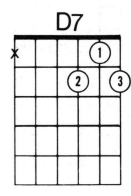

F
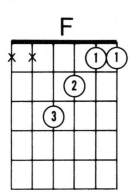

A
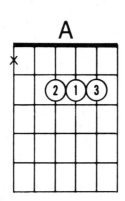

A7
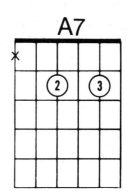

Am
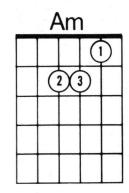

E
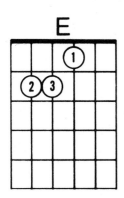

E7
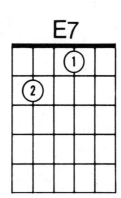

Em
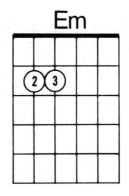

B7
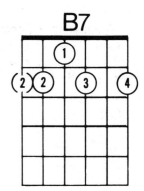

Getting Started

The Left Hand

Here's how you should finger a G chord for most bluegrass playing and for all of the guitar parts in this book:

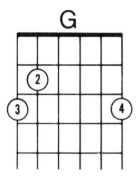

Notice that the fingers are placed close behind the frets. This gives you a clear sound with a minimum of pressure. Be sure to keep your fingers arched at each joint so that all the notes in the chord are free to ring.

The Pick

All the music in this book should be played with a flatpick. Try out the different shapes and sizes until you find one that feels comfortable. Here's a common shape that is good to start with:

A stiffer pick (medium or heavy gauge) will help you get a good bluegrass sound. Hold it firmly, but not too tightly, between your thumb and the side of your forefinger. Keep your hand relaxed, and let your other fingers fall loosely, in a half-curled position.

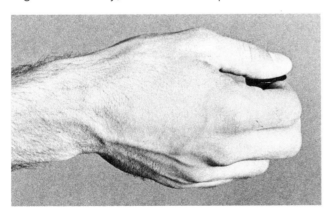

Arm Position

Rest your arm on the side of the guitar so that you're free to move at the elbow. For a good tone, pick the strings over the back part of the sound hole.

When you're just starting to flatpick, it's okay to rest your fingers on the top or pickguard as you play. However, this is a bad habit to continue as your technique develops. It's alright to brush your fingers lightly on the top as you play, but avoid pinning them down rigidly.

Tablature

Tablature is a form of music notation in which the six strings of the guitar are represented by six horizontal lines on a staff. Numbers written on each line indicate which fret to play on each string. This is what a G chord looks like in tablature:

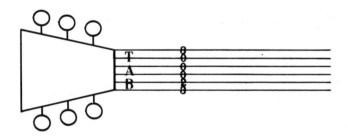

Details of the notation will be explained clearly as we go.

The Basic Bluegrass Strum

Bluegrass accompaniment or backup playing is all based on a basic strumming pattern in which a single bass note is followed by a strum of the chord. Finger a G chord and play the pattern using all downstrokes of the pick. It's written in both standard music notation and tablature.

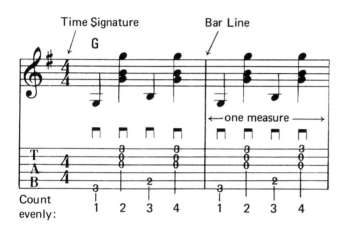

Pick the bass note firmly and clearly. Then strum down across the upper strings. Move with a relaxed motion from your elbow and your wrist and try to get a smooth, even sound when you strum. Notice that within a chord, you alternate back and forth between two different bass notes.

The alternating bass note strum establishes the foundation of the bluegrass rhythm. Try it with these typical bluegrass chord changes. Keep the beat steady and lively.

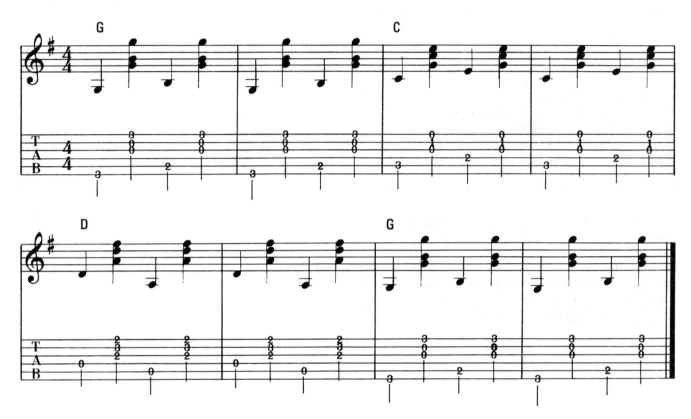

Practice the passage at a slow enough tempo that the chord changes don't cause a break in the rhythm. If a chord change does give you trouble, practice switching back and forth between the chords until you can change in one quick, automatic motion.

A Note on Counting

When you are learning the music in this book, you should count and tap your foot as I described on the previous page. After you've practiced a piece and can play it up to speed, you will tap your foot and feel a strong pulse on the first and third quarter notes of each measure. (You will want to tap your foot only twice per measure.)

For those who read music, this means that the "real" time signature is $\frac{2}{2}$ or ¢.

From here on, the tablature will sometimes use rests to indicate pauses between notes and parts of measures where you don't play.

Rests
- ▬ rest for a whole measure
- ▬ rest for two beats
  (duration of two quarter notes)
- ⸰ rest for one beat
  (duration of one quarter note)
- ⸰ rest for half a beat
  (duration of one eighth note: see p.13)

Make sure you include the rests when you count the rhythm.

Now let's try playing an accompaniment to *She'll Be Comin' Round the Mountain* in the key of D. The upper staff gives the melody in standard music notation. The lower staff has the backup part in tablature.

She'll Be Comin' Around the Mountain

The Double Strum

Most bluegrass backup is played with a double strum in the alternating bass note pattern. It's a simple variation of what you've just learned. Follow each bass note by a strum down and back (up-stroke with the pick) across the upper strings. (V indicates up-stroke.)

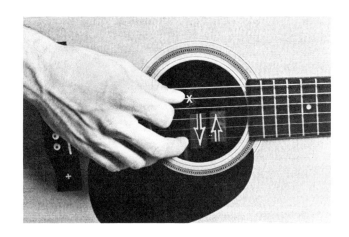

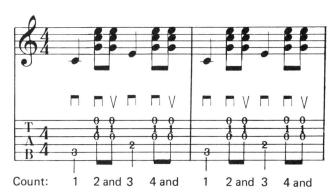

Count: 1   2 and 3   4 and   1   2 and 3   4 and

Eighth Notes

An eighth note lasts half as long as a quarter note. So, there can be two eighth notes per beat, and eight per measure. Groups of two or four eighth notes are written with a single beam connecting their stems, as you can see in the example of the double strum. A single eighth note is written like this: ^{2}

Each part of the double strum is an eighth note, so play both of them evenly in the span of a single beat. The up-strum comes between the beats as you lift your foot between taps and count "and". Make sure the duration of a beat remains constant.

Now here's some double strum backup to *Wreck of the Old 97*.

Wreck of the Old Ninety-Seven

Don't worry too much about hitting exactly three strings on each strum. Aim for a good sound with a snappy beat. Your strums will sound smoother if you keep your wrist and arm relaxed.

Bass Runs

Now you're ready to make your backup playing more musical. We'll start with simple bass runs. These are groups of single notes played on the lower strings. They are used in backup playing to lead from one chord to another.

Try these runs going from C to G and back. Notice that the single notes are all quarter notes, which are played with down-strokes. Release the chords as you play the runs.

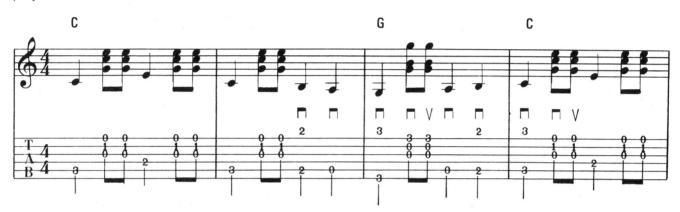

Left-hand Fingerings
When necessary, left-hand fingerings will be indicated immediately above the tablature staff. Occasionally, alternate fingerings will be given in parentheses.

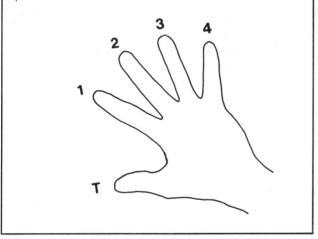

Practice the runs until you can play them with no hesitation. As you play the last note of a run (first note of the next chord), finger the whole new chord so you're ready to strum.

Here are some common runs in the key of G. The one in the third measure adds motion to the music while the chord (C) stays the same.

Now that your hands are feeling more comfortable with bass runs, let's accompany a few familiar songs with guitar parts using some of them. Try to hear the tune in your head (or, better yet, sing or hum it) as you play.

After you learn a guitar part, play it rhythmically and with spirit. Strong and steady backup guitar playing is the cornerstone of good bluegrass.

Oh Susanna

Jesse James

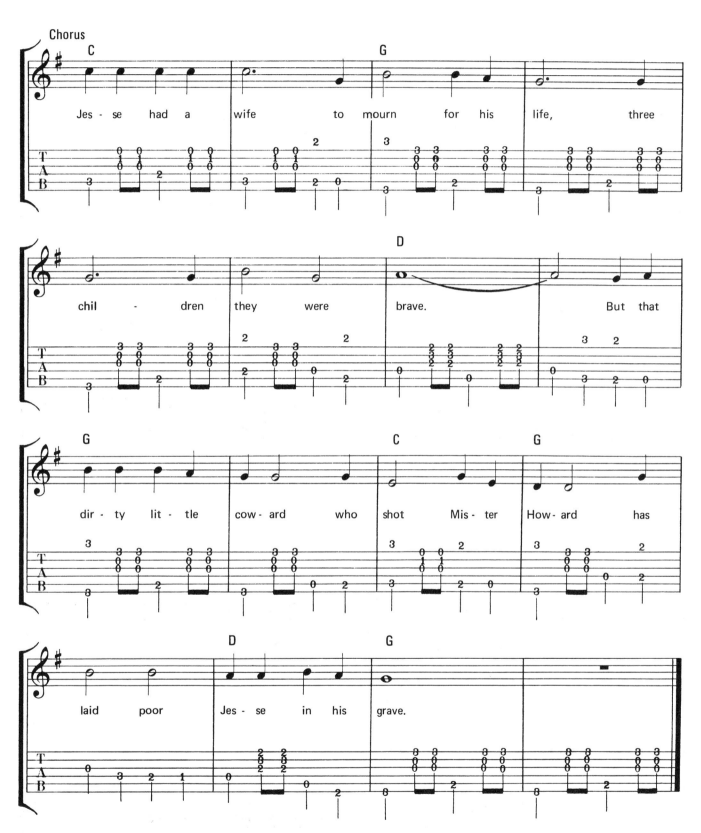

More lyrics on next page

It was on a Wednesday night, the moon was shining
    bright
They robbed the Glendale train.
And the people they did say for many miles away
It was robbed by Frank and Jesse James.

It was on a Saturday night when Jesse was at home
Talking with his family brave,
Robert Ford came along like a thief in the night
And laid poor Jesse in his grave.

Robert Ford, that dirty little coward
I wonder how he feels,
For he ate of Jesse's bread and he slept in Jesse's
    bed
And he laid poor Jesse in his grave.

This song was made by Billy Gashade
As soon as the news did arrive.
He said there was no man with the law in his hand
Who could take Jesse James when alive.

Banks of the Ohio

Play this one at a moderately slow tempo.

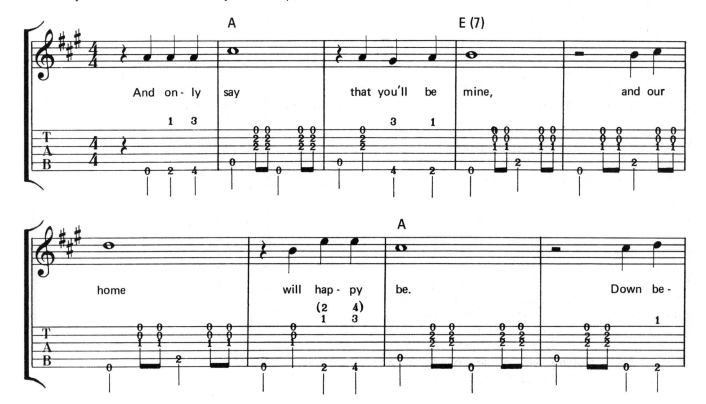

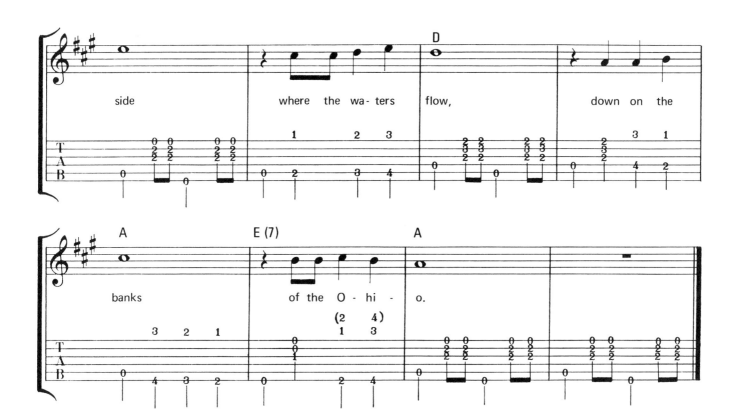

I asked my love to take a walk
Just a walk a little way.
As we walked along we talked
All about our wedding day.

I held a knife close to her breast
As into my arms she pressed.
She cried: Oh, Willie, don't murder me.
I'm not prepared for eternity.

I took her by her lily white hand
Led her down where the waters stand.
There I pushed her in to drown
And watched her as she floated down.

I started home 'tween twelve and one
I cried: My God, what have I done?
I murdered the only woman I loved
Because she would not be my bride.

The very next morning about half-past four
The sheriff came knocking at my door.
He said: Young man, come with me and go
Down to the banks of the Ohio.

Now you should be able to play interesting backup to most any bluegrass song, as long as you know the chords. Don't feel that you have to play a run at every chord change as we did in the last three tunes. (This was done to give you the most practice in the space available.) Simple runs played in well-chosen places make for more effective backup.

Playing Solos

It's just a small step from playing bass runs to playing a melodic bluegrass solo. To play a simple break to a song, you pick the melody with down-strokes and strum when necessary to fill in spaces between the melodic notes.

New River Train is an old country song made popular by Bill and Charlie Monroe in the early days of bluegrass. Let's take a look at the first few measures of the break.

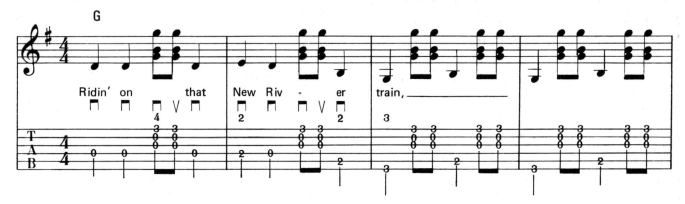

In breaks of this kind, hold down a chord position whenever possible. However, you must release one or more fingers when you need to play a melody note not contained in the chord itself. (For instance, the first note of the second measure.)

Notice that a double strum can occur on any beat, depending on how the melody goes.

Half Notes

The last note of the break to *New River Train* (next page) is a half note. A half note lasts for two beats. In tablature it is written as simply a number (or numbers, in the case of a chord) on the staff. It has no stem. Always play half notes with down-strokes.

New River Train

Chorus:

*More lyrics
on next page*

Darling, you can't love one
Darling, you can't love one.
You can't love one and have any fun
Darling, you can't love one.

Darling, you can't love two
Darling, you can't love two.
You can't love two and still be true
Darling, you can't love two.

The same way:
(three) You can't love three and still love me
(four) You can't love four and love any more
(five) You can't love five and get money from my hive
(six) You can't love six, for that kind of love don't mix

Note: The words are included just for reference, and wouldn't normally be sung while you play the break. You can, however, sing the melody with backup accompaniment and then play your break between verses.

Tips on Playing Breaks

1. The strums should be a little lighter than they would be in backup playing.

2. The melody is the most important thing here, so try to play the single notes cleanly.

3. After you learn the notes, try to make the break sound good. Isolate the hard parts and practice until technical difficulties no longer interfere with keeping a constant rhythm.

The Hammer-on

The hammer-on is a way of producing two notes with just one stroke of the pick. It will lend a distinctive country sound to your playing.

Play the open D string (fourth string). Then bring your second finger down quickly and firmly on the second fret so that the D string keeps ringing on the new note. The symbol h indicates a hammer-on in tablature.

Finger a C chord and play the following phrase. Count carefully and make sure that you're playing even eighth notes with the hammer-on.

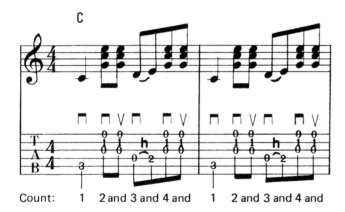

Count: 1   2 and 3 and 4 and   1   2 and 3 and 4 and

Move only your second finger when you hammer-on. Keep the rest of the chord fretted.

Long Journey Home

Long Journey Home is an old bluegrass favorite which will give you some practice hammering-on.

Don't let the last note of the first measure (the hammered note) ring into the second measure.

Release your finger from the D string as you play the first note of the second measure.

When you come to the C chord in measure seven, hammer-on the D string as you finger the whole chord.

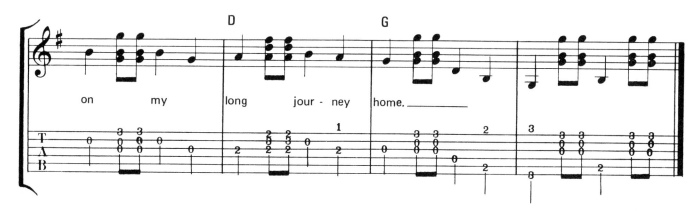

Cloudy in the west and it looks like rain
Looks like rain, boys, looks like rain.
Cloudy in the west and it looks like rain
I'm on my long journey home.

Black smoke a-rising and it surely is a train
Surely is a train, boys, surely is a train.
Black smoke a-rising and it surely is a train
I'm on my long journey home.

Homesick and lonesome and I'm feeling kind of blue
Feeling kind of blue, boys, feeling kind of blue.
Homesick and lonesome and I'm feeling kind of blue
I'm on my long journey home.

Starting into raining and I've got to go home
Got to go home, boys, got to go home.
Starting into raining and I've got to go home
I'm on my long journey home.

The next tune, *Red Wing,* is a familiar country instrumental that you may recognize as the melody to Woodie Guthrie's song, *Union Maid* ("There once was a union maid, who never was afraid"...etc.) This break involves lots of single note playing.

Repeat Signs

When a section of music is enclosed by these signs, you are to repeat that section once, then go on.

These signs indicate first and second endings to a repeated section of music. When you come to them, play only the first ending. Then repeat the section indicated. This time through, skip the first ending and play the second. Then go on.

Red Wing

The Pull-off

This is another left-hand technique in which two notes are produced with one pick stroke.

Play the second fret on the D string with your second finger. Then pull your finger up and off the string so that the open D string sounds. Pull it slightly across toward your palm so that you give the string a gentle pluck. Be careful not to hit the G string as you pull-off. The symbol ⌐ indicates a pull-off in tablature.

This phrase contains a pull-off and a hammer-on.

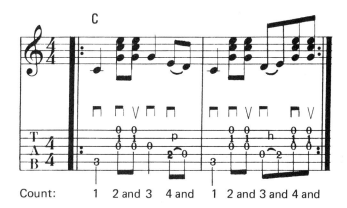

Count: 1   2 and 3 4 and   1   2 and 3 and 4 and

Be sure your second finger is back in place on the C chord for the strum in the second measure.

Here's another bluegrass train song. (I'm sure you'll play a lot more of them before your picking days are over!)

The break uses these two chord forms and will give you a chance to work on pull-offs.

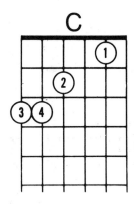
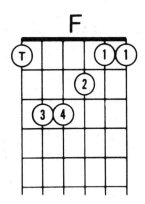

Wabash Cannonball

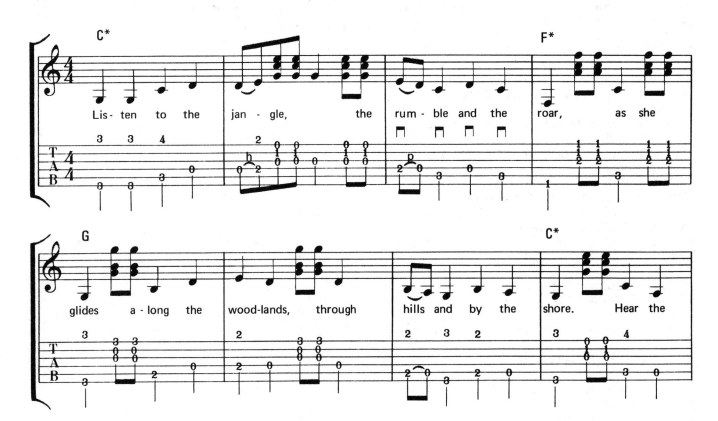

Now the eastern states are dandy
   so the western people say
From New York to St. Louis and Chicago by the
   way,
From the hills of Minnesota where the rippling
   waters fall
No chances can be taken on the Wabash
   Cannonball.

She came down from Birmingham one cold
   December day
As she pulled into the station,
   you could hear all the people say:
Here's a gal from Tennessee, she's long and
   she's tall
She came down to Birmingham
   on the Wabash Cannonball.

Here's to Daddy Claxton, may his name forever
   stand
And always be remembered
   in the courts throughout the land.
His earthly days are over and the curtains
   around him fall
They'll carry him home to victory
   on the Wabash Cannonball.

Using Down-Up Strokes

A lot of bluegrass solo playing involves faster single note runs that contain groups of separately picked eighth notes. To play these runs, you use a down and up motion of the pick.

Start by playing quarter notes in even rhythm, tapping your foot each time you count a beat.

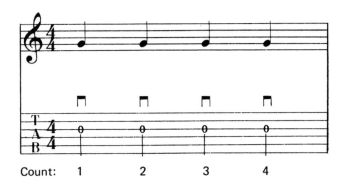

Now, keeping the same beat, play an up-stroke and count "and" after each down-stroke.

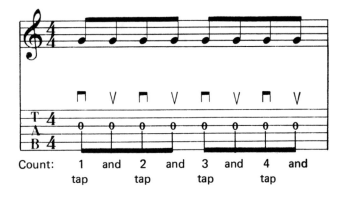

The up-strokes come as you lift your foot between taps. Try to feel as comfortable playing them as you do playing down-strokes. You should be able to play a series of eighth notes evenly with the back and forth motion.

Here's a simple melodic phrase. Repeat the first measure several times without pausing until you can play it smoothly. Put a slight emphasis on the first and fifth notes of the measure.

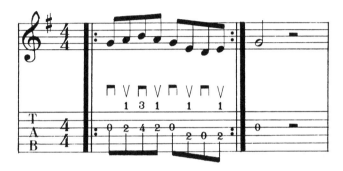

If your fretted notes sound muffled, it may be that the timing is a little off between your left and right hands. Have each note firmly fretted slightly before you pick the string. For a continuous, clear sound, let each note ring right up until the next one is played.

Remember that while groups of eighth notes are played with alternating picking strokes, quarter notes and half notes always get a single down-stroke. Try this phrase:

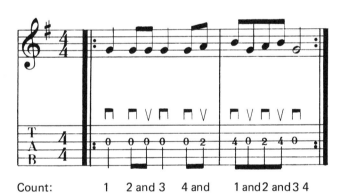

Count: 1   2 and 3   4 and   1 and 2 and 3 4

Since string changes make down-up strokes a little harder, here's an exercise to help smooth them out.

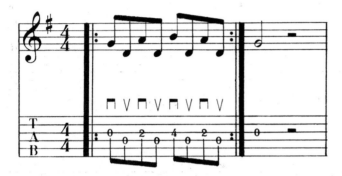

Now let's use the alternating strokes to play some music.

The next three pieces are all old fiddle tunes which lend themselves well to bluegrass guitar breaks. A fiddle tune has two main sections: Part A and Part B. Each part is played twice so that the over-all form is A A B B.

Sally Goodin

This tune is played in the key of A on the fiddle, but best suits the guitar in G. When you play it along with a fiddle or mandolin, a capo on the second fret will put you in the right key.

Divide melodic breaks like this into small sections and practice them phrase by phrase. Watch the fingering!

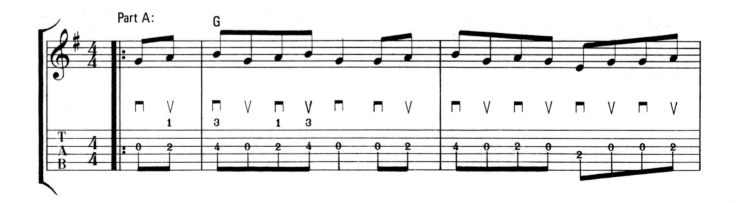

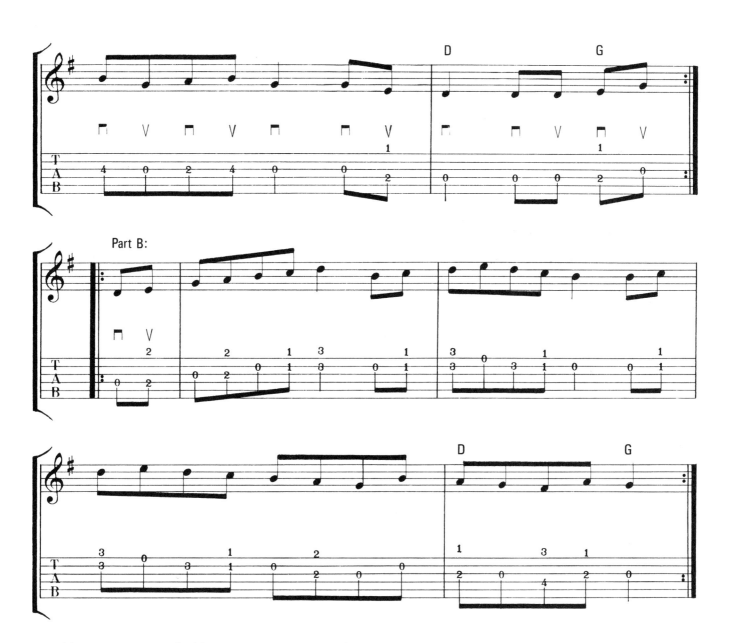

Listen to as much bluegrass as you can to improve your feel for the rhythm. Fiddle tunes originated as country dance tunes, so put some life into them!

Cherokee Shuffle

This next one will give you some good practice playing down-up strokes on the lower strings.

Whenever you flatpick, strive for economy of pick motion. Never "slap" at the strings from too great a distance. Aim for good control.

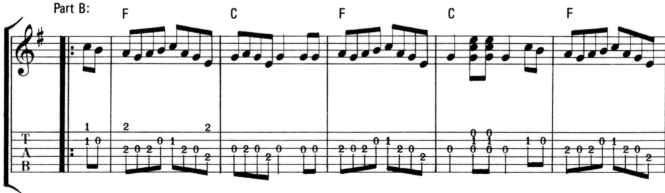

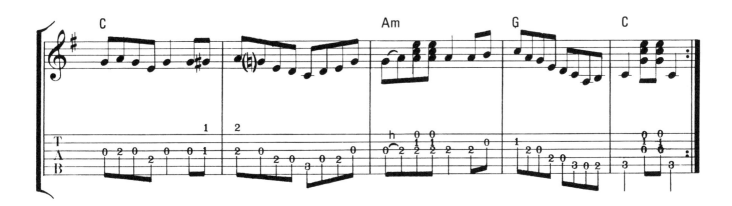

Arkansas Traveller

Here's another old favorite. You'll find your fourth finger called into action in Part B. Watch out when you play backup. The chords move right along!

Remember not to stiffen your right wrist and arm. Now that you're getting used to single note playing, you should also begin to aim for relaxation in your left hand.

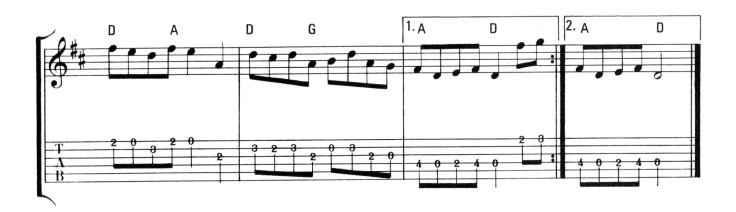

$\frac{3}{4}$ or Waltz Time

Songs which have three beats per measure are said to be in $\frac{3}{4}$ or waltz time. The basic bluegrass backup pattern for these songs is a bass note followed by two double strums.

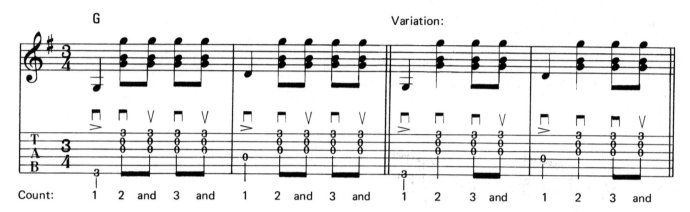

In $\frac{3}{4}$ time there is a strong emphasis on the first beat of each measure.

Here's an old murder ballad with a nice melody and gruesome lyrics.

Down in the Willow Garden

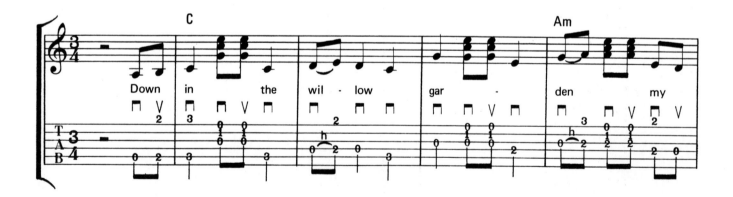

I drew my saber through her, which was a bloody knife
I threw her in the river, which was an awful sight.
My father often told me that money would set me free
If I would murder that dear little girl
    whose name was Rose Connelly.

Now he sits in his cabin door wiping his tear-dimmed
    eyes
Mourning for his only son out on the scaffold high.
My race is run beneath the sun, the devil is waiting for
    me
For I did murder that dear little girl
    whose name was Rose Connelly.

Slides

One last way of producing two notes with one pick stroke is to slide your finger to a new fret after the first note is played. Slides can really add a touch of excitement to your playing.

Hold down the second fret of the G string with your second finger. Play that note, let it ring for a second, then slide your finger quickly to the fourth fret. (Move your hand and arm along, too.) Maintain pressure on the string so that the note on the fourth fret keeps ringing.

Play the following phrase, making sure that the notes involved in the slides get their proper rhythmic value. The symbol ⌒S⌒ indicates a slide in tablature.

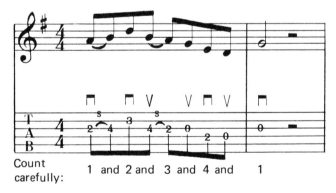

Count carefully: 1 and 2 and 3 and 4 and   1

As a result of the descending slide starting on an off-beat, you play two up-strokes in a row. Hammer-ons and pull-offs can result similarly in successive up-strokes.

Observe this rule of pick direction:

Pick Direction

Notes which start on a beat are played with down-strokes. Those which start on the second eighth note of a beat (the "and" of the beat) are always played with up-strokes.

So, there is a basic connection between the motion of your pick and the rhythm of the notes. You normally move down on the beats and up on the off-beats.

You can also play a slide as simply a quick approach to a note.

In the next phrase, the note at the second fret indicates the starting point of the slide. Pick the string on the down-beat (first beat of the measure) and slide to the fourth fret instantly.

Count: 1 and 2 and 3 and 4 and

The next song, *Roll on Buddy,* is about as blue-grassy as they come. The solo has some interesting runs and slides to add embellishment and spice things up. You'll find the straight melody to the song, along with a backup part and more lyrics, on pages 48 and 49.

This tune is usually played at a fast tempo, but you should take it as slow as necessary to play the break well. Don't ever sacrifice a good sound just to play fast.

Roll On, Buddy

Chorus:

More on Backup

Backup is an important part of bluegrass guitar playing. Now that you've gotten some more skills under your belt, let's take a look at what you can do to give your backup playing a good bluegrass sound.

Varying the Strumming Pattern

To add interest to your playing, vary the backup pattern now and then. For example, combine the regular double strum pattern with a triple strum after the next bass note:

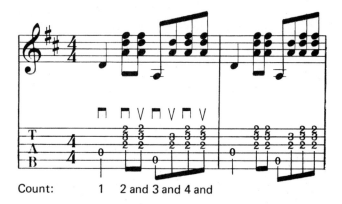

Count: 1   2 and 3 and 4 and

In the triple strum, just hit one or two strings in the up-strum following the bass note. This sounds good in songs like *Banks of the Ohio* and *Wreck of the Old 97*, that aren't too fast. It can also be used occasionally in faster tunes.

You'll find more variations of the backup pattern in the chapter on "Tied Notes and Syncopation."

The Flatt Run

This run (named after Lester Flatt) is *the* most common bluegrass guitar lick, and will give you the bluegrass flavor you've been craving.

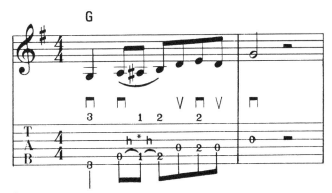

*Hammer—on twice after picking the string once.

The run should be very rhythmic and punchy. It's commonly used as "punctuation" in the gaps between vocal phrases (and similarly in instrumentals). As you will see in the backup part to *Roll on Buddy*, it can also be used as an ending for a song.

There are many forms of the Flatt run. Here are a couple of the common variations:

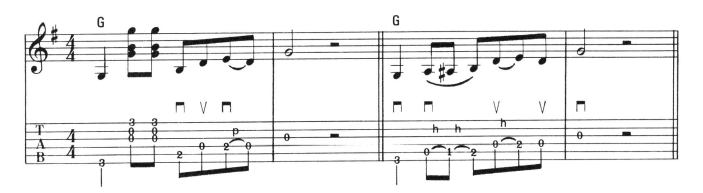

This backup part makes typical use of Flatt runs. There are also some triple strums and new bass runs using down-up strokes.

Roll On, Buddy

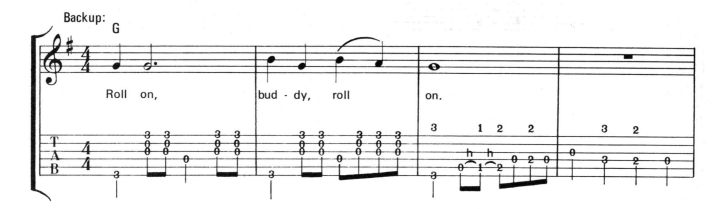

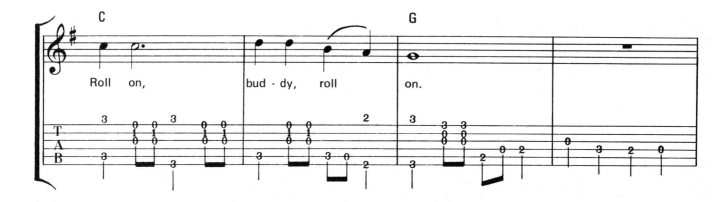

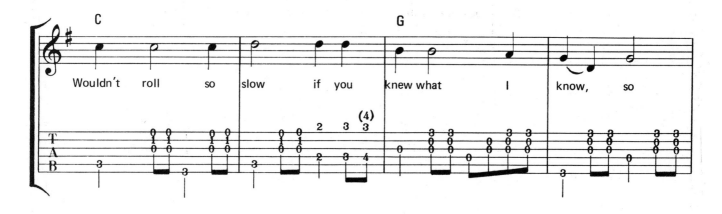

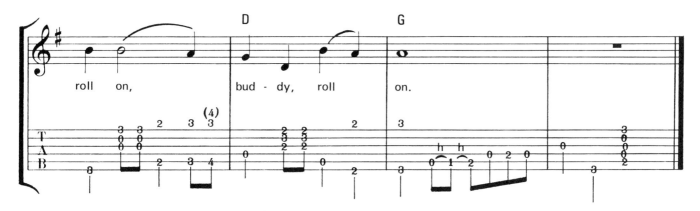

roll on, bud - dy, roll on.

I'm going to that east pay road (2x)
I'm going to the East, I'm going to the West
I'm going to the one that I love best.

My home is down in Tennessee (2x)
In sunny Tennessee, that's where I want to be
Way down in sunny Tennessee.

I've got a good woman just the same (2x)
Got a woman just the same,
    and I'm gonna change her name
I've got a good woman just the same.

Flatt runs are most commonly played in G, but
they can be played on other chords as well:

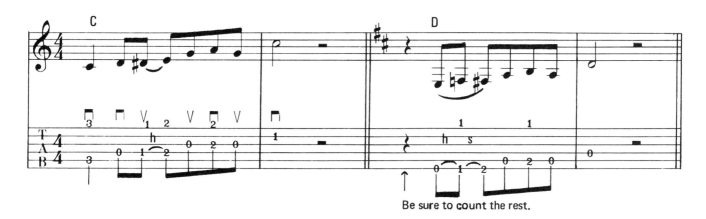

Be sure to count the rest.

Tied Notes and Syncopation

When two of the same notes are tied with an arch (⌒), play a single note that has their combined rhythmic value.

For instance, this is a single note that has the same duration as a quarter note (one beat).

An interesting rhythmic effect results when a note is started on the second eighth note of one beat and is tied over into the next beat. First play this simple bass run going from G to D:

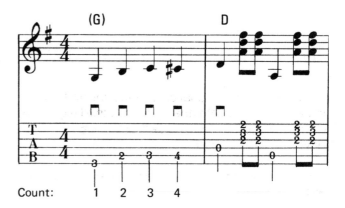

Now try this rhythmic variation of the same run:

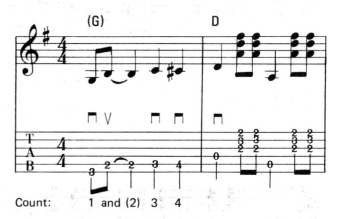

By changing the accent of the beats in the run, you get a more exciting rhythm—very welcome in bluegrass. Shifting the accent to the off-beat is called syncopation.

Syncopated runs often use successive upstrokes. Try this one:

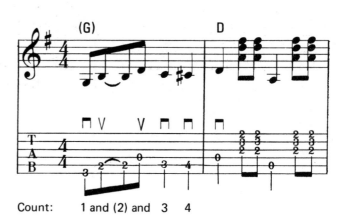

If you have trouble with the rhythm, first play the tied notes as two separate notes:

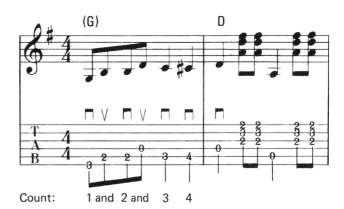

Now play the original phrase with the tied note. Try to hear the extra note (the un-picked third eighth note of the measure) in your head as you eliminate the down-stroke and hold the longer note.

Try this passage of backup containing bass runs with syncopations:

Here are two strumming patterns that use tied notes and syncopation. Use them occasionally to spruce up your backup.

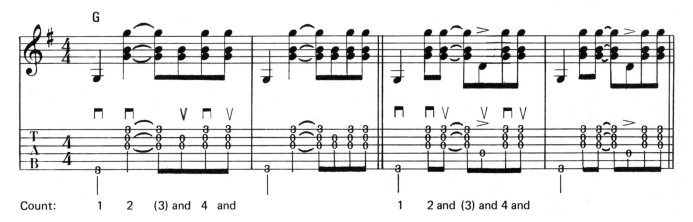

Count: 1   2   (3) and 4 and   1   2 and (3) and 4 and

Example B is tricky. But notice that all you're doing is delaying the second bass note in each measure until the off-beat after its normal place on the third beat.

Watch for syncopation in some of the upcoming solos.

Congratulations! You've come a long way and now should have all the basic technique you need to play bluegrass well. Just play as much as you can, and you'll find that your control, speed, and agility will all steadily improve.

This last group of tunes should give you plenty to work on as you sharpen up the skills that you've learned so far. They're exciting solos that will also introduce you to some slightly more advanced picking situations. When you can play them well, you'll really be an excellent flatpicker.

More Tunes

Red-Haired Boy

Also known as *Little Beggarman*, this piece was originally an Irish fiddle tune. It'll be the first break you've learned in the key of A.

John Henry

John Henry went upon the mountain
His hammer was striking fire.
But the mountain was too tall, John Henry was too
    small
So he laid down his hammer and he died, Lord, Lord,
Laid down his hammer and he died.

John Henry went into the tunnel
Had his captain by his side.
The last words that John Henry said:
Bring me a cool drink of water 'fore I die, Lord, Lord,
Cool drink of water 'fore I die.

John Henry had a little woman
And her name was Polly Ann.
John Henry took sick and he had to go to bed
Polly drove steel like a man, Lord, Lord,
Polly drove steel like a man.

Talk about John Henry as much as you please
Say and do all that you can.
There never was born in the United States
Never such a steel-driving man, Lord, Lord,
Never such a steel-driving man.

John Henry told his captain:
I want to go to bed.
Lord, fix me a pallet, I want to lay down
Got a mighty roaring in my head, Lord, Lord,
Mighty roaring in my head.

They took John Henry to the graveyard
And they buried him under the sand.
Now every locomotive comes-a-roaring by
Says: Yonder lies a steel-driving man, Lord, Lord,
Yonder lies a steel-driving man.

Billy in the Lowground

In *Billy in the Lowground* you'll get a chance to do some crosspicking. Crosspicking is a repeated, rolling picking pattern across three neighboring strings. Let's take a look at the first line of Part B:

For the crosspicking in the third and fourth measures of the example, finger a D chord position at the fifth fret. You are actually playing an F chord. It'll take a good stretch to play the eighth fret with your fourth finger while you hold down the chord position.

As you crosspick, keep your wrist relaxed and mobile. It's a very difficult right-hand technique, so don't be discouraged if it doesn't come right away.

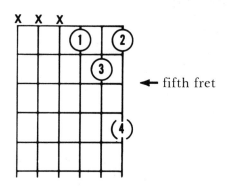

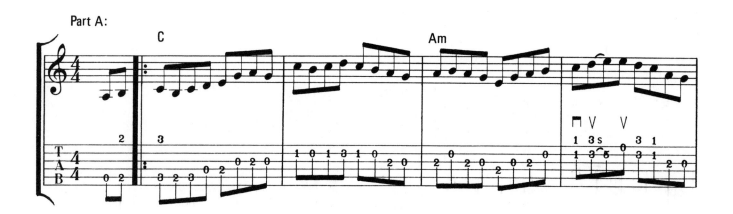

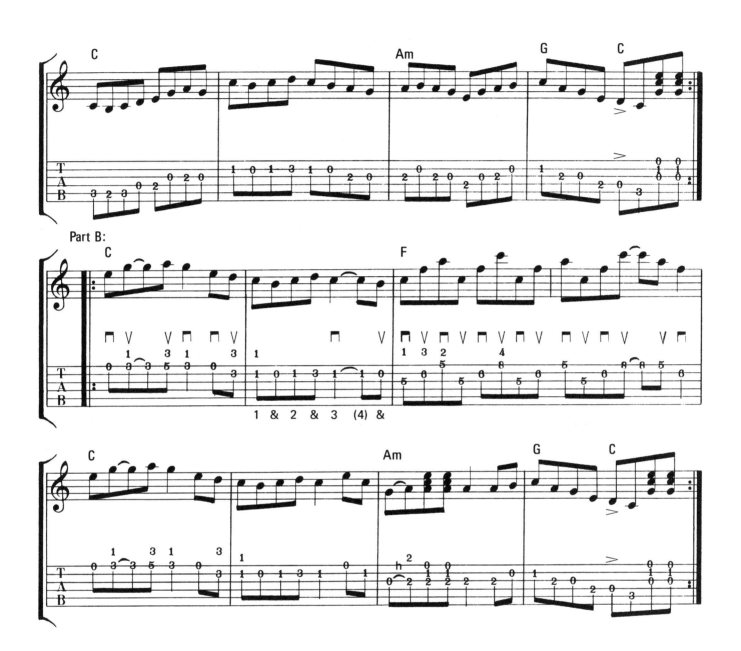

Mountain Dew

Here's another interesting solo that's built around a simple, well-known melody. Watch your pick direction and count carefully!

In the eighth measure, you play and slide two notes at once. Pick both strings in one quick motion so that they ring at the same time.

The first line of music is a fiddle-style lead-in lick that introduces the break.

Bascomb Lunsford, Scott Wiseman

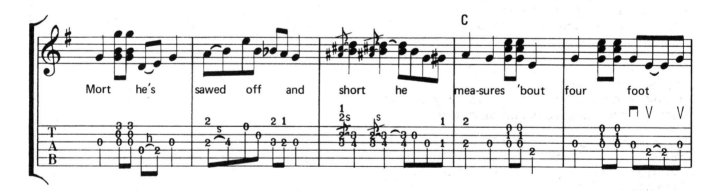

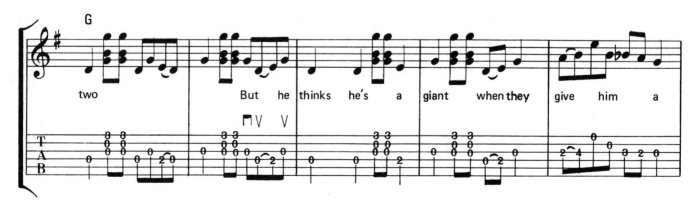

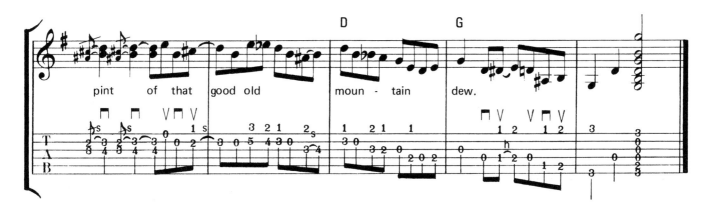

Chorus:
They call it that old mountain dew
And them that refuse it are few;
I'll hush up my mug if you fill up my jug
With that good old mountain dew.

More verses:

My Aunty June's got a brand-new perfume
It has such a sweet-smelling pu.
Imagine her surprise when she had it analyzed
Turned out to be that good old mountain dew.

The preacher came by with a tear in his eye
He said that his wife had the flu.
We said that he ought to give her a snort
Of that good old mountain dew.

Mr. Roosevelt told me just how he felt
The day the whiskey law ran through.
He said if your liquor's red it will swell up your head
Better stick to that good old mountain dew.

My Uncle Bill's got a still on the hill
Where he'll run off a gallon or two.
The birds in the sky get so drunk they can't fly
From smelling that good old mountain dew.

New Camptown Races

New Camptown Races was written as a mandolin tune by Frank Wakefield. It makes a terrific guitar instrumental. This version includes a pretty flashy ending lick.

Frank Wakefield

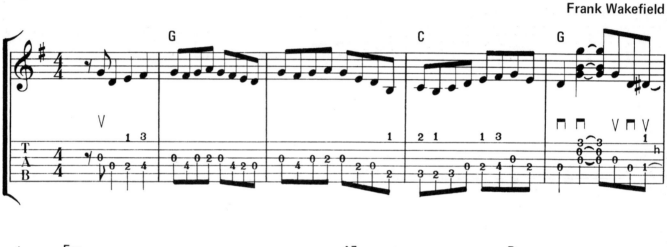

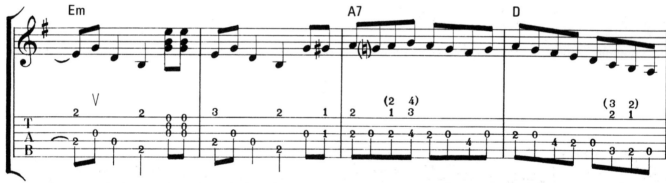

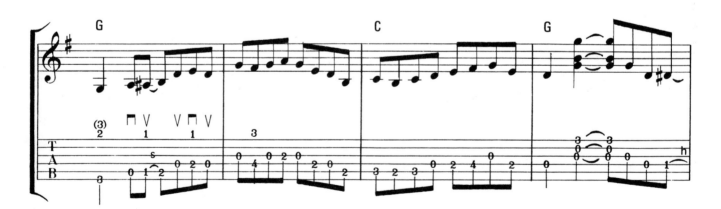

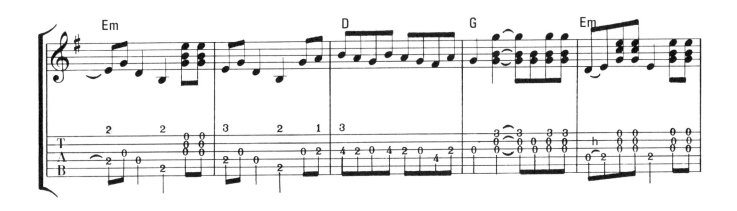

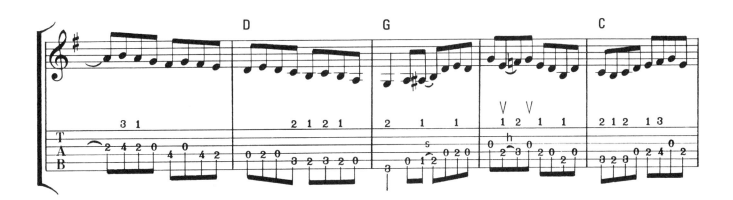

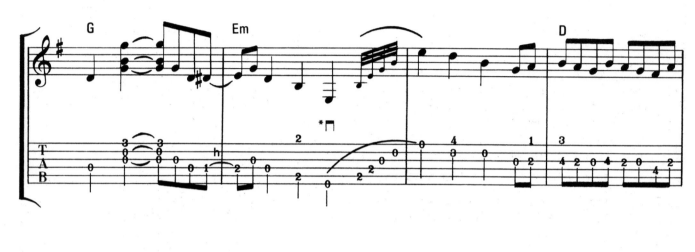

*Start to strum the full E minor chord on the last beat of the measure. Draw out the strum a little so that each note rings an instant after the preceding one. Finish rolling the chord as the next measure begins, emphasising the high E string as a melodic note on the downbeat. This embellishment has a brilliant and startling effect.

Appendices

Using a Capo

A capo allows you to change the key of a song without changing the fingerings or chord positions you use to play it. It's fairly common to use a capo in bluegrass music for the following reasons:

1) To change the key to suit your vocal range.

2) To play in a certain key to match other instruments.

3) To get a specific effect as a result of playing higher or lower on the neck with particular chord positions.

Here's a chart showing what key you'll be in with the capo on various frets:

PLAY CHORD POSITION FOR:	ACTUAL KEY WITH THE CAPO:				
	Off	on 1st fret	on 2nd fret	on 3rd fret	on 4th fret	on 5th fret
G	G	Ab	A	Bb	B	C
C	C	Db	D	Eb	E	F
A	A	Bb	B	C	D	D
D	D	Eb	E	F	Gb (F#)	G
E	E	F	Gb (F#)	G	Ab	A

Suggested Listening

Country Cooking (with Russ Barenberg)
Country Cooking Rounder 0006
Barrel of Fun Rounder 0033

Dan Crary
Lady's Fancy Rounder 0099

J. D. Crowe (with Tony Rice)
J. D. Crowe and the New South Rounder 0044

Lester Flatt and Earl Scruggs
The Golden Era Rounder Special Series 05

Jim and Jesse
Bluegrass Classics
Bluegrass Special
(both out of print, but terrific if you can find them)

Jimmy Martin and the Sunny Mountain Boys
Good N' Country MCA 81

Bill Monroe and the Bluegrass Boys
Bluegrass Style Coral Records CB-20077
Bluegrass Time MCA 116
Bluegrass Instrumentals MCA 104

Reno and Smiley
Country Tunes King 701

Tony Rice
Tony Rice Rounder 0085

The Stanley Brothers
Everybody's Country Favorites King 690

Doc Watson
Doc Watson Vanguard VSD 79152
Doc Watson & Son VSD 79170

Clarence White
*The Kentucky Colonels—
Appalachian Swing!* World Pacific 1821 (out of print)
The Kentucky Colonels 1965-1967 Rounder 0070
The White Brothers Live in Sweden 1973 Rounder 0077